Self-development

through the Eightfold Path

ISBN: 978-1-7354372-0-0 (eBook)

ISBN: 978-1-7354372-1-7 (Paper Print)

ISBN: 978-1-7354372-2-4 (Hardcover Print)

Self-development through the Eightfold Path

Minh Tam Dewey

I am grateful to

- **Dr. Elise A. DeVido** for her editing

- **Dr. Nguyen Quoc Tuan** for his giving the foreword

- **Dr. Damien Keown** for his giving the title to my book

CONTENTS

Foreword

Dr. Nguyen Quoc Tuan, the Late Director of the Institute For Research On Religions in Hanoi

****

There are many ways to learn the Buddha's teachings, and the author's method is one of the various ways to practice Buddhist lessons. Although this is a piece of work, it is pregnant with her experience in studying Buddhist philosophy. I am sure that if a person like her is going on the path to Buddhism and gains knowledge of the Buddha's teachings, then her labor will be perfect.

One day, she realized that she had still "lost her way" even though she had taken refuge with the Buddha for a long time. Now, she must strive to learn again His teachings right away, learning in the light of wisdom and compassion that the Buddha has taught us. Based on her understanding and experience, she knew she needed to learn how to love, live and let live, forgive and forget, drive all selfishness and hatred away, and fix her imperfections in which everyone is quickly immersed.

Following the twists of fate in her life, she presents the order: Precepts –> Concentration -> Wisdom. As we know, there are many ways to understand Buddhist philosophy. One's karma is a primary factor affecting Buddhist philosophy's understanding. Therefore, depending on their own karma, people can follow a way to reach Buddhism. The Eightfold Path is an effective method that people should practice to clear their minds of illusions that are likely to make people think they are unique and then fall into misleading.

The Eightfold Path is not just a talk; this is a great lesson. Practicing the Buddha's words is quite as difficult as we wade upstream. As a lay devotee, the author has kept the precepts and gone to the next steps. Due to her karma, she describes her work in a simple way but remains to adhere to the Buddha's and Patriarch's teachings. Of course, "wading upstream" may cause her to practice Buddhist philosophy harder. However, being determined to improve herself, she no longer loses her way.

This book not only discusses personality but also presents the perfection of personality that achieves success in self-development through the Eightfold Path.

I wish to share my understanding with the author and readers.

Hanoi, Nov. 8th, 2006

Preface

In 2006, I wrote an article about my attempt to study Buddhism after a long period of straying from the path. At the time, I had hoped to submit the article to the Buddhist University in London as part of my application for a master's degree, but unfortunately, my application was unsuccessful. However, a professor at that University did me a favor by giving me the title of my book. I was so grateful to him. Consequently, the article was later transformed into a book published in Vietnam, though its content remained incomplete.

It has now been reprinted in the US, and I have endeavored to edit and supplement it with additional content based on my practical experiences.

However, I remain cautious about delving too deeply into the significance of the Eightfold Path, as my primary aim is to present Buddhism in a simple and accessible manner for readers who may be new to Buddhist philosophy.

The Eightfold Path is a critical practice towards Enlightenment, a challenging journey for many practitioners. The profound nature of the Eightfold Path necessitates diligent effort from practitioners, a task daunting for us as ordinary individuals. Therefore, this book endeavors solely to assist ordinary people in cultivating their own personality through a simplified presentation of the philosophy under the ultimately noble meaning of the Eightfold Path. Yet, I aspire for everyone to embark on a journey toward truth, goodness, and beauty through self-improvement to benefit themselves, others, and society.

In the past, I often complained about my life, which seemed filled with tribulations. I felt distraught and could only see the negative aspects of life - how harsh it could be and how unkind people seemed. I convinced myself that I was being mistreated by both my family and life. However, the more I tried to justify my feelings, the more pain I experienced.

One day, I realized that despite having taken refuge with the Buddha for a long time, I had still lost my way. It was because I had never turned over every single word of the Buddha in my mind. I supposed that His teachings were only for monks who strive to attain Enlightenment, while human beings like me could not understand or practice. Maybe I always found faults with others without feeling sympathy for them.

People, by nature, are imperfect. The division between the spirit of evil and good in man is as thin as a hair. We cannot deny that this is true. However, if human beings' nature tends towards the good, they are likely to improve themselves. In this way, the present work is for my wish to improve myself and to express sympathy for those who have the same misunderstanding about the Buddha's teachings. His words are always a torch to light the way of the Sangha (monastic community), lay followers, and even people who know very little of Buddhist philosophy.

From time to time, we are told that the sutras are beyond our understanding. Only people who have perfect wisdom can understand them. Are all human beings wise enough to thoroughly grasp the sutras? Then they practice reaching Enlightenment? That is why we feel apprehensive about studying His teachings. Frankly speaking, we should only ponder over his simple words, for example:

"Don't lead a life of indulgence. Don't perform a despicable act. Don't support a wrong view. Don't make the world worse."[1]

In order not to exacerbate the situation but to lead a righteous life, we must conquer ourselves. It is

[1] Dhammapada (para. 167)

because "Victory in battle is easier than triumphing over oneself. Being victorious in the battle against yourself is the most significant triumph in your life."[2]

Now, both you and I can fully understand the significance of these simple yet resolute words. If we commit to practicing His teachings every day, even in small increments, we will increasingly nurture our spirit of goodness. Through this spirit of goodness, our personality will be strengthened and affirmed.

However, it is pretty difficult for us to improve ourselves because, by nature, we can scarcely recognize our mistakes. We tend to support our views while finding others' perspectives unsound. Thus, if we are too cowardly to achieve victory for our common sense, we are still trapped in the delusion of grandeur.

Therefore, from now on, "we should no longer exacerbate situations, no longer find fault with others,

---

[2] Dhammapada (para. 103)

and no longer comment on their actions."[3] Instead, We should focus on identifying our faults and reflecting on our actions. Moreover, We should consider that "Being a victim of glaring injustice serves as an effective method of self-development."[4]

May this work be dedicated to all sentient beings advancing their understanding. Later, everyone will earnestly strive to practice the Noble Eightfold Path, with the ultimate aim of attaining Enlightenment.

Reprinted in Virginia, USA, in 2024

---

[3] Dhammapada (para. 50)
[4] Samadhiraja Sutra

I. Introduction

Since the Buddha passed away, His teachings have spread all over the world. Over an extended period, His ideology has penetrated people's thoughts from all social classes. His philosophy, influenced by everyone's karma and the teachings of various Buddhist schools, has been studied, analyzed, and applied to human life.

Motivated by the strange twists of fate in my own life, my present work will be a study of **Self-development through the Eightfold Path.**

When "Self-development through the Eightfold Path" is mentioned, one might assume that it refers to the Sangha's Self-development. However, it is not solely about this aspect. Self-development through the Eightfold Path, which both Sangha and lay followers can realize, is presented in this work. It is not only reflected in the Sangha's precepts but also expressed through one's behavior. This is the path of spiritual practice following the Eightfold Path. The present study focuses on the cultivation of virtue in individual persons and does not delve deeply into the Sangha's transcendent ideology.

Actually, the Eightfold Path is the noblest path to Enlightenment. However, it is pretty challenging to attain Enlightenment as we are everyday individuals living in luxurious surroundings and modern industrial society. For the sake of argument, let us assume that the Eightfold Path is a saintly way of life that we can practice refining our own personality.

Advancing our personality toward perfection means that we are enhancing our lives to achieve true happiness in our present life. The Buddha once said, "The Eightfold Path that I have shown will lead you to a secure and peaceful life."[5]

---

[5] Referring to "Majjhima Nikaya-Dvedhavitakkasutta," translated into Vietnamese by Reverend Thich Minh Chau

What is the Eightfold Path (Atthangikamagga)?

According to the Comprehensive Study of Buddhism, the Eightfold Path refers to the eight paths or eight effective methods that guide people to a perfect life.[6] In the Dhammapada, the Buddha said, "The Eightfold Path is the holiest way."

The Eightfold Path is divided into three groups:[7]

- Precepts (Sila)
- Concentration (Samadhi)
- Wisdom (Prajna)

---

[6] Comprehensive Study of Buddhism (Phat Hoc Pho Thong), Chief Editor Thich Thien Hoa, p.479.

[7] In the Chinese Madhyama Agama and the Pali Majjhima Nikaya, a Comparative Study, p.98, Reverend Thich Minh Chau noted, "Does the noble eightfold path include the three groups, or the three groups include the noble eightfold path? The Noble Eightfold Path does not include the three groups, but the three groups include the Noble Eightfold Path. Right speech, right action, right livelihood, these three constituents are included in the noble moral precept group; right mindfulness, right concentration, these two constituents are included in the noble concentration group; right view, right aspiration, right means, these three constituents are included in the noble wisdom-group. This is why the Noble Eightfold Path does not include the three groups but the three groups include the Eightfold Path".

Precepts, known as Sila, are the rules that guide people on how to conduct themselves with dignity and cultivate their virtue. Buddhists who strictly observe the Five Precepts (Pancasila) can refine their character. The Precepts are the beginning of emancipation, or the beginning of concentration, and the arising of wisdom, including the Right Speech, the Right Action, and the Right Livelihood.

Concentration, known as samadhi, is a method that guides people in practicing achieving mental balance and self-control. When feelings and the mind are stable, one can determine precisely what to do and how to act. A person's correct actions can reveal his excellent character. Samadhi includes the Right Effort, the Right Mindfulness, and the Right Concentration.

Wisdom, known as Prajna, is what helps people realize their bad habits, prejudices, or wrong views so that they can end them. Wisdom is a good guide that leads people toward a life of virtue. In the Upasaka Sutra, the Buddha said, "Wisdom distinguishes humans from animals." Wisdom enables people to judge their actions and to take responsibility for their behavior. Wisdom includes the Right View and the Right Thought.

In a lecture on the Four Noble Truths, Venerable Thich Chan Quang emphasized, "Every single action in the Eightfold Path is always to bring happiness to people and lessen their suffering. If people completely practice the Eightfold Path, they can stop being in the samsara. This reminds us of correctly practicing the Eightfold Path."[8]

Thus, we firmly believe that those who earnestly practice the Eightfold Path will experience profound changes in their lives, leading to complete happiness. By diligently following this path, individuals can enhance their personal development and refine their personalities.

---

[8] Referring to the lecture of Ven. Thich Chan Quang on the Four Noble Truths

What is personality?

In this context, "personality" refers to individuals characterized by virtuous behavior and exemplary moral conduct. As one's character and conduct are cultivated through proper training, one's personality is further developed.

When a child is born, they inherently possess wisdom and disposition. As they grow up, they gradually become good or bad, better or worse, depending on their education and environment. Therefore, education and the environment have a critical effect on the development of people's character. Parents must realize how important it is to find a suitable method and approach for their children's education.

Parents should thoroughly grasp the Buddha's teachings, which are helpful in training their children to have good character and educating them to be good individuals for their family and society.

In addition to showing the Sangha a way to Enlightenment, the Buddha clearly depicted how they could perfect their character and conduct in accordance with the standards of Buddhist philosophy. The Eightfold Path is what people should practice to improve their personality and guide their children later on.

****

II. Self-development through the Eightfold Path

A. Self-development through the Right View (Samma Ditthi)

The Right View is accurate perception and awareness grounded in objective reality. It requires us to observe and comment without the influence of personal biases or cultural prejudice. Those who, upon the Right View, consistently discern between right and wrong.[9]

The Right View emphasizes the importance of having precise understanding and awareness to affirm our personalities. For example, to offer insightful commentary on our surroundings, we must possess practical observational experience and a comprehension of moral principles. Without such experience and understanding, our perspectives on reality may lack coherence. The Right View encompasses both practical experience and knowledge, serving as a crucial element in the cultivation of our personalities.

---

[9] Comprehensive Study of Buddhism. Ven. Thich Thien Hoa. P. 480

The Right View is paramount in Buddhist practice because it serves as the foundation for all other aspects of the path to Enlightenment. Some stories below can illustrate its significance.

The Blind Men and the Elephant is a famous parable that tells of several blind men who encountered an elephant for the first time. Each touched a different part of the elephant and formed a different interpretation of what an elephant was like based solely on their limited experience. One perceived the elephant as a wall (touching its side), another as a spear (touching its tusk), and so on. They argued vehemently, each insisting that their view was correct. However, none of them had the complete picture until someone with sight came along and described the elephant. This story highlights the importance of having a comprehensive understanding (the Right View) to avoid misunderstandings and conflicts.

The Poisoned Arrow, another Buddhist parable, narrates that a man was shot with a poisoned arrow. Instead of seeking immediate medical attention, he demanded answers to questions about the arrow's origin, the materials used to make it, and the archer's identity. By the time he received this information, he had succumbed to the poison and died. This story underscores the urgency of addressing immediate concerns, such as suffering, rather than becoming preoccupied with speculative questions. The Right View encourages us to focus on what is essential for our spiritual growth and liberation from suffering.

The tale of Anasrava, an Enlightened One, offers a poignant illustration of the significance of the Right View. Anasrava was a monk of remarkable talent and righteousness, traits that aroused jealousy among his peers, even his own master. One fateful day, his master, consumed by envy, tasked Anasrava with committing a heinous act of murder under the guise of attaining Enlightenment.

Blinded by obedience and lacking discernment between right and wrong, Anasrava tragically succumbed to his master's command. His actions led to his arrest, instilling fear and unrest. In his ignorance of the Right View, he became an instrument of suffering, inflicting anguish upon others. It became evident that his misdeeds had eroded his very essence.

However, fate intervened when Anasrava encountered the Buddha. Through the Buddha's teachings, Anasrava found Enlightenment, dispelling the darkness of ignorance that had clouded his judgment. In embracing the Right View, he discovered the path to true understanding and liberation from suffering.

The Four Noble Truths, the foundation of the Buddha's teachings, begins with the Right View. Understanding the nature of suffering (the first truth) and its causes (the second truth) requires a clear and accurate perception of reality. Without the Right View, one may misinterpret suffering or its origins, hindering progress toward liberation.

In the Dhammapada, we are reminded that discerning right and wrong constitutes the Right View, serving as the guiding light for humanity. This ability to navigate ethical choices illuminates our personal growth and development path.

The Buddha's quest for the truth serves as a profound example of the Right View. After devoting six years to the rigorous ascetic practices of monkhood, the Buddha realized that such extreme austerity did not lead to Enlightenment. Instead, it only depleted the body, rendering the mind susceptible to impurities. The ascetic lifestyle, marked by relentless self-denial, failed to cultivate the necessary conditions for Enlightenment.

Through his own experience, the Buddha discovered that true Enlightenment transcends the extremes of asceticism. Rather than through self-mortification, Enlightenment arises through a balanced and mindful approach to spiritual practice. By nurturing a clear and tranquil mind, free from the disturbances of extreme asceticism, one paves the way toward genuine realization and liberation from suffering.

The Right View illuminated the path to truth for the Buddha, serving as a timeless beacon guiding humanity towards righteous living for millennia. It remains the paramount lesson for daily practice, enriching and refining our personalities.

In the Kalamasutta, the Buddha imparted wisdom, advising that belief and action should be grounded in personal experience and truth and that happiness should be promoted for oneself and others.

In essence, cultivating the Right View stands as one of the most effective methods for discerning between right and wrong. Through this clarity, we gain insight into how to conduct ourselves with integrity and virtue. Good behavior becomes a hallmark that enriches and uplifts the value of our personalities.

In summary, the Right View is indispensable because it provides the correct understanding and perspective for navigating life's challenges and progressing toward Enlightenment. These stories illustrate the practical implications of cultivating the Right View and the pitfalls of misunderstanding or neglecting its importance.

****

B. Self-development through the Right Thought (Samma Samkappa)

The essence of the Right Thought lies in clear and upright thinking. Those who diligently practice the Right Thought conscientiously contemplate their actions, remain mindful of harmful or unwholesome thoughts, and willingly acknowledge them through confession.

In a lecture on the Four Noble Truths, Venerable Thich Chan Quang emphasized that the Right Thought encompasses profound contemplation on life, Dharma, and correct practice, all of which stem from accumulating the practice of the Right View.[10]

Those who consistently reflect upon their misdeeds and openly confess them triumph over their inner turmoil. This process is the most effective means of refining people's characters and attaining personality perfection.

---

[10] Referring to the lecture of Ven. Thich Chan Quang on the Four Noble Truths

The Buddha imparted His wisdom to His son Rahula: "When you think about the bad things you have done, you should confess to your master, mentor, or fellow practitioners. Through this practice, you can prevent relapsing into your misdeeds while purifying your body, mind, and speech."[11]

Those who adhere to the Right Thought contemplate virtuous actions and strive to abandon detrimental habits. Their minds remain steadfast, unclouded, and evil thoughts as they conscientiously engage in mindful speech and actions toward others.

According to Venerable Thich Chan Quang, the Right Thought contains many points; one of them is to think of goodness, which leads people to behave gently toward others, animals, the environment, and society. Goodness is a small sphere but more practical and specific.[12]

---

[11] Referring to "The Buddha and His Teaching," written by Narada, translated into Vietnamese by Pham Kim Khanh

[12] Referring to the lecture of Ven. Thich Chan Quang on the Four Noble Truths

Deliberating on the Buddha's teachings, they integrate these profound insights into their daily lives, ensuring their thoughts never harm anyone. Embracing the Right Thought serves as yet another avenue for enhancing and refining one's personality.

Out of compassion for humanity, the Buddha pledged to liberate us from the cycle of rebirth, known as samsara. This profound commitment arose during His time as the Crown Prince, igniting His relentless pursuit of Enlightenment.

Reflecting on our actions, if we earnestly contemplate the troubles we inflict upon our loved ones or strangers and sincerely repent for our wrongdoings, we can bring joy to others. Alternatively, nurturing a sense of responsibility towards our families and contributing positively to society can foster happiness and well-being.

We cultivate virtues that enrich our personalities by prioritizing the prosperity of our lives, families, and communities.

In my perspective, embracing the Right Thought serves as a potent catalyst for personal growth and improvement.

In essence, the practice of the Right Thought entails thoughtful contemplation of our lives and the phenomena around us, enabling us to discern the most beneficial course of action for personal betterment. Through careful reflection on our deeds and words, we gain the ability to assess ourselves accurately. Our capacity for correct thinking serves as a reflection of our personality. Therefore, cultivating the Right Thought becomes indispensable in elevating the quality and value of our personalities.

****

C. Self-development through the Right Speech (Sammavaca)

In the *Comprehensive Study of Buddhism*, the Right Speech is defined as honest, fair, straight, and reasonable words (Ven. Thich Thien Hoa, p. 481). It is vital that one adheres to these principles to improve one's personality.

Additionally, the Right Speech entails refraining from speaking ill, lying, and boasting. Refraining from speaking ill involves avoiding insults or verbal abuse toward others. Avoiding lies means telling the truth, as the truth possesses inherent strength and value, leading to positive outcomes. Abstaining from boasting involves not excessively praising oneself or flaunting one's knowledge to assert superiority over others.

However, in order to cultivate these qualities, individuals must strive to refine themselves. They may not hesitate to deceive others because of wealth, fame, or sentiment. They may also deflect responsibility for their mistakes by attributing them to others. Alternatively, to avoid hurting friends or relatives, they may refrain from discussing their mistakes with them. Therefore, the meaning of the Right Speech encompasses not only honesty, fairness, and straightness but also sensible and skillful communication.

Individuals with a boastful disposition like to show off how great their abilities are. Their speech, unintentionally or intentionally, may hurt or make others jealous. In addition, they are likely to speak ill of others, viewing it as a way to "prove" themselves as better people. In reality, their hurtful words naturally contribute to a negative character.

One of the Five Precepts of Buddhists is "Do not lie." However, "do not lie" does not only mean "not telling a lie" but also implies "not uttering bad speech." Therefore, the Right Speech should be understood in a flexible sense, allowing people to apply it reasonably in various situations.

The Buddha stated, "There are five manners of talking to others: timely or untimely, true or untrue, kind or unkind, useful or useless, with love or resentment." [13]

In the Dhammapada, the Buddha said, "Do not speak cruelly to anyone. People insult others, and others respond in kind. A sharp tongue truly hurts others. A war of words is as hurtful as actual wounds."[14] He also reminded his disciples as follows:

> Prevent your words from being angry.
>
> Train your words in kindness.
>
> Cease the evils of your words.
>
> Let your words be gentle.[15]

The Buddha advised Maha Moggallana that he should never engage in discussion that would lead him to lengthy

---

[13] Referring to "Majjhima Nikaya Sutra (Kakacupamasutta)," translated by Reverend Thich Minh Chau, p. 291

[14] Dhammapada, para. 133

[15] Ditto, para. 232

conversations, agitation, a disturbed state of mind, and hinder the achievement of meditation (Jhana).[16]

In His final teachings, the Buddha reminded the Sangha to refrain from indulging in meaningless chatter. This illustrates that the Buddha did not want His disciples to fall into the error of engaging in frivolous conversation, let alone resorting to sharp language.

It is often said that courtesy costs nothing, so one should be courteous when speaking to each other. Elders always advise the younger generation to think carefully before uttering a word. A paragraph in the Dhammapada mentioned the Right Speech as follows:

> Cruelly speaking to people,
>
> or treating them with disdain
>
> is a kind of karma
>
> in which a grudge will be nursed.

---

[16] Referring to "Maha Moggallana," by Hellmuth Hecker, translated into Vietnamese by Nguyen Dieu

Speaking to people in a soft voice
or treating them with respect
is a kind of karma
in which calm will enter, and hatred will go away.
Living in the world,
Man should get to know
that a tongue with which man abuses each other,
is like a knife that a man uses to cut himself.[17]

In summary, the Right Speech holds significant importance in cultivating virtues essential for personal growth. By practicing the Right Speech, individuals uphold ethical standards and foster qualities such as empathy, compassion, and integrity. Moreover, the Right Speech helps to promote harmonious relationships, enhances communication skills, and builds trust and respect within communities. Ultimately, the mindful use of language not only reflects one's character but

---

[17] Referring to "Stories of Dhammapada," compiled by Bhikkhu Thich Minh Quang

also plays a pivotal role in shaping this individual; thus, the Right Speech is really a cornerstone of ethical living and personal development.

****

D. Self-development through the Right Action (Samma kammanta)

The Right Action is defined as those correct actions that adhere to accepted standards or rules and benefit all living creatures.[18]

The Right Action follows the Right Speech, actively promoting and reinforcing the principle advocated in the Right Speech. As Venerable Thich Chan Quang aptly stated, "If the Right Speech advocates for charity, then the Right Action promotes actively charitable deeds."[19] This alignment underscores the importance of translating words into actions, ensuring that ethical principles are not merely spoken but lived

---

[18] Idem, P.482

[19] Referring to the lecture of Ven. Thich Chan Quang on the Four Noble Truths

out practically. Thus, the Right Action complements and extends the impact of the Right Speech, fostering a harmonious integration of ethical conduct into daily life.

Additionally, a correct action by itself demonstrates that one's personality is well-trained. People can assert their personalities through their proper actions. Being mindful of their deeds, they always consider whether their actions will conform to societal standards, cause harm to others, or should be undertaken.

When people are assigned tasks, they strive to do their best and take responsibility for their jobs. In doing so, they conduct themselves with dignity, a characteristic of a perfect personality.

When speaking of the Right Action, the Buddha reminded us that a wise person does not engage in evil deeds for oneself, others, children, wealth, career, or power. A virtuous individual never resorts to unethical means to achieve success. These people adhere entirely to the Buddha's teachings.[20] In the Dhammapada, the Buddha also mentioned the five precepts of Buddhists: By living a life that leads to committing killing, theft, adultery, alcohol consumption, and lying, people undermine their personalities in the present life.[21]

The five precepts serve as guiding principles for Buddhists and anyone who wants to improve themselves. They offer a framework for ethical conduct and moral behavior. Beyond mere prohibitions, they represent a pathway toward cultivating inner harmony and spiritual growth.

The precept against killing is to avoid harm but promote compassion toward all living beings. It encourages mindfulness in our actions and fosters our empathy and respect for life in all its forms. Refraining from stealing emphasizes a life of honesty in which individuals express respect for others' property. Those who adhere to this principle uphold their moral actions. Preventing adultery not only avoids causing harm to others but

---

[20] Referring to "Reading Dhammapada of Hinayana" by Reverend Thich Tri Quang. Para. 84

[21] Ditto, Para. 246-247

also ourselves. Upholding this precept fosters trust, stability, and mutual respect within relationships, leading to ethical actions. Abstaining from intoxicants avoids making people trouble. This precept keeps individuals aware of their actions, promoting health, well-being, and spiritual development. The precept against lying underscores the importance of honesty, integrity, and transparency in communication. This precept guides individuals in cultivating trust, authenticity, and clarity in their actions.

When the Buddha encouraged people to engage in good deeds to counteract their wrongdoings, He said, "Whoever, by a good deed, covers the evil done, such a one illuminates this world like the moon freed from the clouds."[22]

In the Dhammapada, the Buddha reminded us, "If people speak good and do good, Merit will follow them. Good deeds make merits. An act of kindness will bring peace."[23]

---

[22] Dhammapada Para. 173, complied by Ven Narada

[23] Referring to "Stories in Dhammapada," complied by Ven. Thich Minh Quang, published in 1995

The present work does not delve into the law of karma because Buddhist philosophies are primarily based on the law of karma. Instead, it focuses solely on analyzing the characteristics of personality.

When people act kind, they will feel peaceful, as they have just cultivated their virtues. These virtues reaffirm their excellent personalities.

Doing good deeds does not merely connote charity; sometimes, people may engage in charitable acts not out of genuine concern for others' needs but rather for their fame or personal benefit. As discussed here, the essence of doing good deeds lies in performing acts of kindness without expecting any benefit in return. Furthermore, such actions benefit people and society, aligning with societal standards and ethical principles.

When Prince Rahula was only seven years old and a novice monk, his father, the Buddha, taught him, "Before undertaking any action, you should carefully consider whether your acts hurt you or others, leading to worry and suffering.

Such actions should be avoided as they are deemed wrong. Conversely, if your actions ensure neither harm nor suffering but instead foster peace and happiness for yourself and others, they are considered righteous deeds and should be done. [24]

The Buddha's teachings are invaluable in helping people discern right and wrong actions. Following His teachings, people can cultivate awareness and ensure their actions consistently align with goodness. Ultimately, their adherence to the Right Action contributes to developing a perfect personality.

****

[24] Referring to "The life of the Buddha," by Ven. Thich Minh Phat

E. Self-development through the Right Livelihood (Samma Ajìva)

The Right Livelihood was understood as an honest occupation to earn one's living. Those who adhere to the Right Livelihood principles earn their livelihood honesty, ensuring that their wealth is not amassed at the expense of others' labor and that they do not cause suffering to humans or animals through their work.

One who lives by the Right Livelihood lives a meaningful life: doing himself and others benefit, doing an honest day's work, never living a parasitic life (Ven. Thich Thien Hoa, p.482).[25]

The characteristics of the Right Livelihood that one should achieve to perfect their personality are as follows:

In the Angutara-Nikaya, the Buddha consistently emphasized the importance of earning an honest living to His lay followers. He conveyed that those who adhere to the Right

---

25 Comprehensive Study of Buddhism, p. 482

Livelihood and the Right Action legally accumulate wealth through effort, talent, and virtue. Such individuals ensure their wealth is utilized for their sustenance, their families' support, and others' welfare.[26]

Thus, officials who engage in corruption unjustly amass wealth through the labor of others. Similarly, if a building contractor prioritizes greed over integrity by skimping on materials, his construction, such as roads, bridges, or buildings, is undoubtedly of inferior quality. The resulting infrastructure, such as roads, bridges, or structures, will likely be substandard. This negligence can lead to costly repairs or catastrophic collapses, causing loss of lives and intensive damage.

The ill-gotten wealth of drug dealers, smugglers, liquor vendors, and arms dealers is built upon others' suffering. A worker who shirks honest labor does not deserve their wages. Likewise, employers who fail to provide fair compensation for a

---

[26] Referring to "Sudattanathapindika," written by Hellmuth Hecker, translated into Vietnamese by Nguyen Dieu

day's work exploit their employees. Parasitic individuals squander their lives in idleness, contributing nothing of value to society.

The individuals described above lack personality, integrity, and moral character. Contrasting them with those who adhere to the Right Livelihood provides a clear basis for comparison. Living by the Right Livelihood enables individuals to demonstrate their personalities by leading a meaningful life. They engage in actions that benefit both themselves and others. They perform honest work and refrain from living parasitically off society. Living by the Right Livelihood allows individuals to cultivate a solid and admirable personality founded on virtue and ethical conduct.

According to the Buddha's teachings, there are four kinds of happiness, one of which is associated with the Right Livelihood: true happiness arises when one achieves wealth through diligent effort and honest means. Such individuals experience a profound sense of fulfillment, knowing their earnings are acquired with integrity. Therefore, those who earn their living honestly will obtain inner peace and happiness. Living by such principles makes their virtuous characters evident, leading to continuous improvement and enhancement of their personalities.

When discussing livelihood, it is essential to acknowledge the livelihood of monks, which lay followers support. Unlike ordinary people, monks do not earn their living through conventional means. Instead, they rely on the generosity of others. However, their steadfast commitment to upholding the precepts and preserving the Dharma is a profound example for Buddhists.

Venerable Narada eloquently depicted the Buddha's life, illustrating how He tirelessly preached throughout the day, devoting merely an hour to sleep.[27] The Buddha's existence was dedicated to the liberation of humanity, exemplified by His

---

[27] Referring to "The Buddha and His Teachings," translated by Pham Kim Khanh-Thuan Hoa Publishing House

unwavering commitment to saving beings. His life serves as a beacon, guiding us in building our livelihood with purpose and integrity.

In conclusion, embracing the right livelihood benefits society and facilitates the perfection of our personalities. We contribute positively to the world through ethical and meaningful work while cultivating inner growth and development.

****

F. Self-development through the Right Effort (Samma Vayama)

The Right Effort entails individuals exerting themselves to bring about goodness for themselves, others, and animals. Those who adhere to the Right Effort consistently strive to better themselves, remaining resolute in performing virtuous deeds while actively rejecting unwholesome thoughts.

Those who adhere to the Right Effort constantly improve themselves, striving to do good deeds and resolving to reject evil thoughts (Ven. Thich Thien Hoa, p. 483).[28]

By exploring the Four Right Efforts (Samyakprahana) in greater depth, one can grasp the characteristics that contribute to enhancing one's personality. Let us delve into each of these efforts.

Indeed, the Four Right Efforts can be summarized as follows:

Preventing the arising of evil: Through diligent effort, one strives to avoid unwholesome thoughts, emotions, and actions from arising in the mind. By cultivating mindfulness and awareness, individuals can intercept negative tendencies before they manifest into harmful behaviors.

Putting an end to existing evil: With sustained effort, individuals work towards eradicating any existence of unwholesome qualities or behaviors within themselves. This

---

[28] Comprehensive Study of Buddhism, p. 483

involves recognizing and acknowledging harmful patterns and actively seeking to overcome them through introspection, self-discipline, and practice.

Bringing goodness into existence: Through intentional effort, individuals actively cultivate virtuous thoughts, emotions, and actions. They engage in practices that promote kindness, compassion, generosity, and other positive qualities, thereby fostering a wholesome inner state and contributing to the well-being of others.

Developing existing goodness: Individuals endeavor to strengthen and enhance their wholesome qualities with dedicated effort. This involves nurturing positive traits such as wisdom, patience, mindfulness, and empathy through consistent practice, reflection, and cultivation. By deepening their virtuous qualities, individuals contribute to their growth and the welfare of society.

By diligently applying the Four Right Effort, individuals can gradually transform themselves, developing a more compassionate, virtuous, and balanced personality.

Indeed, the Right Effort serves as an effective method for nurturing and refining our personalities. The story of novice monk Rahula's morning vow exemplifies the profound commitment to inner cultivation, as he aspired to develop his mind with the same dedication as the handful of sand he tossed into the air.[29] Despite his young age of seven, Rahula's earnest determination to cultivate himself resonates deeply, inspiring us to engage in the practice of self-improvement similarly.

"The Discipline of a Boddhisattva" emphasizes that individuals who possess self-control and courage and approach themselves and others with equanimity exemplify the essence of the Right Effort. Such individuals selflessly dedicate themselves to the well-being of others, embodying the

[29] Referring to "The Life of the Buddha," written by Ven. Thich Minh Phat

principles of compassion, empathy, and altruism. By embracing the Right Effort in our daily lives, we can foster greater harmony within ourselves and extend compassion towards all beings, thus contributing to the cultivation of a noble and virtuous personality.[30]

In the Dhammapada, the Buddha said, "It is easy to do evil and useless things, but it must make efforts to do good and useful things." (para.163). the Buddha emphasized the inherent difficulty in doing good and valuable deeds compared to the ease of engaging in evil and futile actions. This observation underscores the natural selfish tendencies of human beings. Acknowledging the presence of evil in the world and the challenges associated with resisting it, it becomes evident that striving to bring about goodness for oneself and others is a noble pursuit. Through dedicated efforts to do good, individuals

---

[30] Referring to "The Discipline of A Boddhisattva," by Bhikkhu Thich Tri Sieu

can undergo a transformative process, leading to the reform and refinement of their personalities.

In summary, to effectively practice the Right Effort for the purpose of improving our personalities, it is essential to carefully study and reflect upon the Buddha's teachings as follows:

> Life is too short; all things are impermanent.
> You should be aware that the world is a fool's paradise,
> You should try to cultivate your mind,
> To unseal your eyes and train yourselves in diligence,
> To keep yourselves from defilement,
> And to shed light on your way.
> He was a wise man loving himself.
> Shows diligence in self-improvement,
> Strives for diligence in doing good deeds,
> He never gives up on his improvement.[31]

---

[31] Referring to "Stories of Dhammapada," compiled by Ven. Thich Minh Quang

****

G. Self-development through the Right Mindfulness (Samma Sati)

The Right Mindfulness entails remembering righteousness and sacred teachings that benefit oneself and others. By consistently embodying these principles, individuals can strengthen their moral character and affirm their personality. Let us explore how the meanings of the Right Mindfulness contribute to personal development in more detail.

Virtue and Awareness: Those who cultivate the Right Mindfulness become virtuous by consistently aligning their actions with righteousness and sacred doctrines. This awareness of ethical principles guides their conduct and fosters integrity in their character.

Observation and Self-Control: Through the practice of Right Mindfulness, individuals develop the capacity to observe their thoughts, emotions, and behaviors with clarity and nonjudgmental awareness. This heightened sense of self-awareness enables them to recognize unwholesome tendencies and exercise control over their actions, leading to more excellent emotional stability and self-mastery.

Improvement of Personality: By honing their power of observation and self-control, individuals enhance their personality and character. They become more attuned to their inner workings and better equipped to navigate life's challenges with wisdom and serenity. This continual refinement contributes to the development of a noble and virtuous personality.

Indeed, the practice of the Right Mindfulness serves as a powerful tool for self-development, as it cultivates virtue, enhances self-awareness, and fosters greater control over one's thoughts and actions. By embodying the meanings of the Right Mindfulness, individuals can affirm their personality and strive toward realizing their highest potential.

Reverend Thich Tri Quang's explanation of the Right Mindfulness emphasizes its role in cultivating correct thinking, self-discipline, and concentration.[32] The Right Mindfulness facilitates self-awareness and self-assertion, enabling individuals to remain focused and attentive to their thoughts, emotions, and actions. Buddhists are continuously reminded of their commitment to the Buddhist path through the practice of the Right Mindfulness, while all individuals are reminded of their shared humanity. This recognition of one's identity and spiritual journey serves as a guiding principle for living with integrity, compassion, and wisdom.

From this, we can fully comprehend that people should cultivate the characteristics of the Right Mindfulness to improve their personalities.

When one's mind goes deep into concentration, one will realize clearly the truth that shows them the way to a holy life. They are aware of how good or bad their actions are. Their awareness of doing good deeds perfects their personalities.

---

[32] Referring to Reading Dhammapada of Hinayana volume 1, p.214

As we know, when a mind is concentrated, wisdom will arise. Wisdom is essential for one to be aware of all factors and aspects involved. One can correctly assess the effects of these situations and then find ways of solving them. It is the Right Mindfulness that shows them the right way to follow so they can assert themselves.

In His final teachings, the Buddha emphasized the importance of maintaining the Right Mindfulness, stating that if His disciples consistently upheld this practice, their spiritual growth would remain steadfast. In the Dhammapada, He advises, "Cultivate the Right Mindfulness to keep your mind on the correct path. Make diligent efforts to abstain from wrongdoing."

Why did the Buddha emphasize the avoidance of evil? Because engaging in harmful actions often comes naturally to humans, whereas pursuing goodness requires considerable effort. Additionally, the inclination toward malevolence exists within the human psyche. Thus, it is imperative to remain vigilant about the consequences of our actions in order to avert negative results. Our actions shape our characters, leading to personal transformation.

Finally, the Right Mindfulness plays a crucial role in attaining peace and concentration of the mind. It is from this state of tranquility and samadhi that wisdom emerges. With wisdom, we gain the ability to control our actions and speech. When our actions are guided by kindness, and our words are spoken gently, it reflects our mastery over ourselves. Thus, the Right Mindfulness stands as one of the fundamental paths toward refining our character and achieving personal growth.

****

H. Self-development through the Right Concentration (Samma Samadhi)

The Right Concentration refers to a mental state focused on a valid object that aligns with the truth and benefits both oneself and others. When the mind is only concentrated on good deeds, such as giving love to all living creatures or engaging in activities beneficial to oneself and others, one's virtuous conduct is greatly appreciated. This virtue serves as a reflection of one's character.

The Right Concentration serves as a beneficial mental exercise, akin to physical workouts for the mind. Within the Sangha, it stands as the paramount path to Nirvana. For lay-Buddhists, it provides essential mental conditioning. As we dedicate time to physical exercise for bodily health, nurturing the mind's tranquility is equally imperative. In today's fast-paced world, stress, frustration, fear, and worry easily destabilize our minds. The Right Concentration serves as a remedy, clearing mental clutter and fostering clarity. With pure minds, our moral compass guides us toward righteousness and justice.

Concentration is an inherent quality of the mind, crucial for maintaining equilibrium. As the Buddha proclaimed, “The mind is the forerunner of all states.” Hence, cultivating a tranquil mind fosters stability. With a stable mind, one’s understanding expands effortlessly, enabling astute management of life’s intricacies. Moreover, practicing the Right Concentration greatly enhances effectiveness in daily life.

First, regular practice of the Right Concentration can sharpen cognitive abilities such as focus, attention, and memory. This heightened mental acuity improves problem-solving skills and increases productivity in daily tasks. Second, individuals can develop greater emotional resilience by training the mind to remain focused. This means being better equipped to handle stress, anxiety, and other negative emotions that may arise in daily life. Third, through the practice of the Right Concentration, individuals become more attuned to their thoughts, feelings, and behavioral patterns. This heightened self-awareness fosters personal growth and self-improvement as individuals gain insights into their strengths, weaknesses, and areas for development. Fourth, as mental clarity and stability are cultivated through the Right Concentration, practitioners are better able to discern their core values and principles. This alignment with their values strengthens integrity and authenticity, leading to a more purposeful and meaningful life. Fifth, when people cultivate inner balance and stability, they become more present and attuned in their interactions with others. This deepens connections and fosters empathy and compassion, as they can understand and relate to the experiences of others on a deeper level. Sixth, the daily practice of the Right Concentration equips people with inner resources to navigate their life's challenges with resilience and grace. Instead of being swept away by external circumstances, people develop their capacities to maintain a sense of inner calm and perspective, even in the face of adversity. Seventh, the Right Concentration serves as a powerful tool for deepening spiritual awareness and insight. Through sustained practice, people may experience moments of profound clarity and transcendence, leading to a deeper understanding of the nature of reality and their place within it.

In summary, this understanding makes it evident that the daily practice of the Right Concentration fosters mental balance and stability. This, in turn, cultivates virtuous behavior and fortifies our character and personal development.

****

III. Conclusion

The eight components of the Eightfold Path are intricately interrelated. Practicing concentration helps generate wisdom, which is vital for growing awareness of our lives. The Right Concentration, in turn, flourishes when the body, mind, and speech are purified. Commitment to the Buddha's teachings leads to a virtuous life, wherein virtue becomes its intrinsic reward. By diligently practicing the Eightfold Path, we embark on a journey to refine our personalities and discover genuine happiness within our lifetime.

Legend has it that a king of Hell once questioned the Buddha, "Why should the Earth Treasury Bodhisattva continuously save human beings from their sins when they relapsed into their misdoings in a short time?"

The Buddha replied that humans' bad habits were too challenging to break because they were stubborn and because the spirit of evil in man was unable to destroy.[33]

The Buddha's response reveals that our harmful actions stem from malevolent tendencies. Yet, the Buddha also illuminated the path to self-improvement. The efficacy of this path hinges upon our resolve to transform our habits, thoughts, and actions.

In His parting words, the Buddha said, "You should always make efforts to practice my teachings. If you waste your time now, you will feel regret later. I showed you the best way to a perfect life. It is up to you whether you practice or not."[34]

The Buddha emphasized the importance of diligently practicing His teachings. He cautioned against squandering time, for neglecting spiritual growth leads to regret in the future. The Buddha offered us the blueprint for a fulfilling life, but we

---

[33] Referring to "Shades of Meaning of Earth Treasury Bodhisattva Sutta," by layman Mai Tho Truyen.
[34] Referring to "The Buddha's Last Days and Last Teachings," by Reverend Thich Minh Chau.

are responsible for deciding whether to heed His guidance and embark on the journey towards self-perfection.

It's common to err in our interactions with others, yet we can rectify our behavior by recognizing the inherent value of life. While external influences may bombard us with various perspectives beyond our control, we retain power over our thoughts. We uncover its boundless intrigue and marvel by dedicating ourselves to mindfulness and attentiveness to life's occurrences. This realization prompts us to pursue knowledge, express gratitude for our blessings, and reciprocate kindness with kindness.

The Eightfold Path stands as an effective methodology for refining our personalities. Unlike attempting to control others, which often proves futile, self-improvement lies readily within our grasp. We cannot influence what surpasses our comprehension, but we possess the agency to cultivate ourselves through the Eightfold Path. Thus, it remains incumbent upon us to continually strive for personal growth and development through this transformative practice.

We are expected to err in our interactions with others, yet we can rectify our behavior by recognizing the inherent value of life. There are innumerable sources of views that we cannot control, but we have control over our thoughts. If we spend more time being mindful of what happens, we can realize that life is of endless interest and wonder. We should learn more, be grateful for our blessings, and repay kindness with kindness.

In conclusion, self-development through the Eightfold Path is an effective method for perfecting our personality. Improving ourselves is more accessible than controlling others because it is within our reach. We are unable to do what is beyond our understanding. Self-development through the Eightfold Path is within our reach. Such is the way that we should continuously cultivate ourselves.

Bibliography:

*** One author:**

- Bhikkhu Thich Hoan Quang. *The Buddha's Last Teachings.* Published in 1970.

- Layman Mai Tho Truyen. *Shades of meaning of Ksitigarbha-sutta.* Religious Publishing House, 2006.

- Reverend Thich Minh Chau. *The Chinese Madhyama Àgama and the Pàli Majjhima Nikàya, A Comparative Study.* HCMC Publishing House, 1998

- Reverend Thich Minh Chau. *The Buddha's Last Days and Last Teachings.* Religious Publishing House, 2003.

- Reverend Thich Tri Quang. *Reading Dhammapada of Hìnayàna, volume 1.* Religious Publishing House, 2000.

- Ven. Thich Minh Phat. *The life of the Buddha.* HCMC Publishing House, 1996.

- Ven. Narada. *Dhammapada.* Printed in Taiwan, 2004.

- Zen Master Thich Nhat Hanh. *The Heart of the Sun* (material kept at Xa Loi library)

*** Multiple authors:**

- Ajahn Sumedho, Susanta Nguyen. *The Mind and the Way: Buddhist Reflection on Life.* Religious Publishing House, 2005.

- Hellmuth Hecker, Nguyen Dieu. *Sudattanathapindika.* HCMC Publishing House, 1997.

- Hellmuth Hecker, Nguyen Dieu. *Maha Moggallana.* HCMC Publishing House, 1997.

- Hellmuth Hecker, Nguyen Dieu. *Ananda.* HCMC Publishing House, 1997.

- Hellmuth Hecker, Nguyen Dieu. *Maha Kasyapa.* HCMC Publishing House, 1997.

- Reverend Thich Thien Hoa, Chief Editor. *Comprehensive Study of Buddhism.* Religious Publishing House, 2004.

- Sàntideva, Bhikshu Thich Tri Sieu. *The Discipline of a Boddhisattva,* Published in 1990.

- Reverend Thich Minh Chau. *Majjihima Nikàya (Kakacupama-sutta).* Religious Publishing House, 2003.

- Ven. Narada, Pham Kim Khanh. *The Buddha and His Teachings*. Thuan Hoa Publishing House.

- Ven. Thich Minh Quang translated from the Chinese version. *Stories of Dhammapada.* HCMC Publishing House, 1995.

www.ingramcontent.com/pod-product-compliance
Lightning Source LLC
LaVergne TN
LVHW052054160826
845678LV00015B/3220

* 9 7 8 1 7 3 5 4 3 7 2 1 7 *